# THE
# BARBECUE
# AND GRILL
# BOOK

# THE
# BARBECUE
# AND GRILL
# BOOK

### SIZZLING IDEAS FOR
### DELICIOUS OUTDOOR EATING

## Consulting Editor: Christine France

Sebastian Kelly

First published in 1999 by Sebastian Kelly

© Anness Publishing Limited 1999

Produced by Anness Publishing Limited
Hermes House
88–89 Blackfriars Road
London SE1 8HA

ISBN 1 84081 301 6

*Publisher:* Joanna Lorenz
*Project Editor:* Linda Doeser
*Copy Editor:* Beverley Jollands
*Designers:* Nigel Partridge, Siân Keogh
*Illustrations:* Madeleine David and Lucinda Ganderton
*Front cover:* Lisa Tai, Designer; Thomas Odulate, Photographer;
Helen Trent, Stylist; Lucy McKelvie, Home Economist
*Photographers:* Karl Adamson, William Adams-Lingwood, Edward Allwright,
Steve Baxter, James Duncan, John Freeman, Michelle Garrett, Amanda Heywood,
Don Last, Michael Michaels, Patrick McLeavey, Debbie Patterson and
Juliet Piddington
*Recipes:* Carla Capalbo, Jacqueline Clark, Carole Clements, Roz Denny, Nicola
Diggins, Tessa Evelegh, Joanna Farrow, Christine France, Silvana Franco, Soheila
Kimberley, Ruby Le Bois, Sue Maggs, Katherine Richmond, Steven Wheeler
and Elizabeth Wolf-Cohen

Previously published as part of a larger compendium, *The Ultimate Barbecue Cookbook*

Printed and bound in Hong Kong/China

1 3 5 7 9 10 8 6 4 2

NOTES
Standard spoon and cup measurements are level.
Medium eggs should be used unless specified otherwise.

# CONTENTS

∘ ∘ ∘

# INTRODUCTION

. . .

Cooking outdoors is one of the great pleasures of the summer.
The delicious smell of charbroiling food is almost irresistible,
stimulates the appetite, and—even better—tempts everyone to
help with the cooking.

The recipes in this book are divided into six chapters with
something for all tastes, each course and every occasion. Five-
spice Rib-Stickers, Shish Kebab, Spiced Beef Satay and
Blackened Cajun Chicken and Corn feature among the all-time
favorites, and there are many innovative and unusual barbecue
treats. These include Lamb Burgers with Red Currant Chutney,
Grilled Sea Bass with Citrus Fruit and Grilled Goat Cheese
Pizza. Plenty of vegetarian dishes are included and barbecued
desserts will be a delicious new taste experience for those who
have never thought of charbroiling fruit.

The introductory section of the book is packed with helpful
information to make cooking on a barbecue as trouble-free,
safe and relaxed as possible. It includes advice on the various
types of barbecue, kinds of charcoal and other fuels, safety tips,
cooking times and marinating.

Whether you are planning a family picnic with a disposable
barbecue or throwing a summer party with a sophisticated gas
grill, you will find that cooking this way makes food taste
better while also being fun and easy to prepare.

# CHOOSING A GRILL

There is a huge choice of ready-made grills on the market, and it's important to choose one that suits your particular needs. First decide how many people you want to cook for and where you are likely to use the grill. For instance, do you usually have barbecues just for the family, or are you likely to have barbecue parties for lots of friends? Once you've decided on your basic requirements, you will be able to choose between the different types more easily.

*ABOVE: Hibachis*

### Hibachis

These small cast-iron grills originated in Japan—the word *hibachi* translates literally as "firebox." They are inexpensive, easy to use and easily transportable. Lightweight versions are now made in steel or aluminum.

### Disposable Grills

These will last for about an hour and are a convenient idea for picnic-style barbecues or for cooking just a few small pieces of food.

### Portable Grills

These are usually quite light and fold away to fit into a car trunk so you can take them on picnics. Some are even small enough to fit into a backpack.

### Brazier Grills

These open grills are suitable for use on a patio or in the garden. Most have legs or wheels, and it's a good idea to check that the height suits you. The grill area of a brazier varies in size, and the brazier may be round or rectangular. It's useful to choose one that has a shelf attached to the side. Other extras may include an electric, battery-powered or clockwork spit: Choose one on which you can adjust the height of the spit. Many brazier grills have a hood, which is useful as a windbreak and gives a place to mount the spit.

*LEFT: Brazier grill*
*BELOW: Disposable grill*
*RIGHT: Portable grill*

ABOVE: *Gas grill*

ordinary house bricks, but it's best to line the inside with firebricks, which will withstand the heat better. Use a metal shelf for the fuel and a grid at whatever height you choose. Kits are available containing all you need to build a grill.

### Improvised Grills

Barbecue cooking adds to the fun of eating outdoors on picnics and camping, trips but transporting the grill for the rest of the day can make the idea more of a chore than a treat. Basic grills can be built at almost no cost and can be dismantled after use as quickly as they were put together. A pile of stones topped with chicken wire and fueled with driftwood or kindling makes a very efficient grill. Or take a large cookie tin with you and punch a few holes in it; fill it with charcoal and place a grid on top. With just a little planning, you can turn your trip into a truly memorable event.

ABOVE: *Improvised grill*

### Kettle Grills

These have a large, hinged lid, which can be used as a windbreak; when closed, the lid allows you to use the grill rather like an oven. Even large cuts of meat or whole turkeys cook successfully, as the heat reflected within the dome helps to brown the meat evenly. The heat is easily controlled by the use of efficient air vents. This type of grill can also be used for home-smoking foods.

### Gas Grills

The main advantage of these is their convenience—the heat is instant and easily controllable. The disadvantage is that they tend to be quite expensive.

### Permanent Grills

These are a good idea if you often have barbecues at home. They can be built simply and cheaply. Choose a sheltered site that is a little way from the house, but with easy access to the kitchen. Permanent grills can be built with

ABOVE: *Permanent grill*

# TYPES OF FUEL

· · ·

If you have a gas or electric grill, you will not need to buy extra fuel, but other grills require either charcoal or wood. Be sure to choose good-quality fuel and always remember to store it in a dry place.

### *Lump Charcoal*
Lump charcoal is usually made from softwood, and comes in lumps of varying size. It is easier to ignite than briquettes, but tends to burn up faster.

### *Charcoal Briquettes*
Briquettes are a cost-effective choice of fuel, as they burn for a long time with a minimum of smell and smoke. They can take a long time to ignite, however.

ABOVE: *Charcoal briquettes*

### *Self-Igniting Charcoal*
This is simply lump charcoal or briquettes treated with a flammable substance that catches fire very easily. It's important to wait until the ignition agent has burned off before cooking food, or the smell may taint the food.

### *Coconut-Shell Charcoal*
This makes a good fuel for small grills. It's best used on a fire grate with small holes, as the small pieces tend to fall through the gaps.

### *Wood*
Hardwoods such as oak and olive are best for grilling, as they burn slowly, with a pleasant aroma. Softwoods tend to burn too fast and give off sparks and smoke, making them unsuitable for most grills. Wood fires need constant attention to achieve an even, steady heat.

---

### CONTROLLING THE HEAT
There are three basic ways to control the heat of the grill during cooking.

**1** Adjust the height of the grill rack. Raise it for slow cooking, or use the bottom level for searing foods. For medium heat, the rack should be about four inches from the fire.

**2** Push the burning coals apart for lower heat; pile them closer together to increase the heat of the fire.

**3** Most grills have air vents to allow air into the fire. Open them to make the fire hotter, or close them to lower the temperature.

---

### *Wood Chips and Herbs*
These are designed to be added to the fire to impart a pleasant aroma to the food. They can be soaked to make them last longer. Scatter wood chips and herbs straight onto the coals during cooking, or place them on a metal tray under the grill rack. Packs of hickory or oak chips are easily available, or you can simply scatter twigs of juniper, rosemary, thyme, sage or fennel over the fire.

---

### LIGHTING THE FIRE
Follow these basic instructions for lighting the fire unless you are using self-igniting charcoal, in which case you should follow the manufacturer's instructions.

**1** Spread a layer of foil over the base of the grill, to reflect the heat and make cleaning easier.

**2** Spread a layer of wood, charcoal or briquettes on the fire grate about two inches deep. Pile the fuel in a small pyramid in the center.

**3** Push one or two lighters into the fuel or pour about three tablespoons of lighting fluid over it and let sit for 1 minute. Light with a long match or taper and allow to burn for 15 minutes. Spread the coals evenly and leave them to heat for 30–45 minutes, until they are covered with a film of gray ash, before cooking.

BELOW: *Lump charcoal*

BELOW: *Coconut-shell charcoal*

# SAFETY TIPS

. . .

Barbecuing is a perfectly safe method of cooking if it's done sensibly—use these simple guidelines as a basic checklist to safeguard against accidents. If you have never organized a barbecue before, keep your first few attempts as simple as possible, with just one or two types of food. When you have mastered the technique of cooking on a grill you can start to become more ambitious. Soon you will progress from burgers for two to meals for large parties of family and friends.

☆ Make sure the grill is sited on a firm surface and is stable and level before lighting the fire. Once the grill is lit, do not move it.

☆ Keep the grill sheltered from the wind, and keep it well away from trees and shrubs.

☆ Always follow the manufacturer's instructions for your grill, as there are some grills that can use only one type of fuel.

☆ Don't try to speed up the fire—some fuels may take a long time to build up heat. Never pour flammable liquid onto the grill.

☆ Keep children and pets away from the fire and make sure the cooking is always supervised by adults.

☆ Keep perishable foods cold until you're ready to cook—especially in hot weather. If you take them outdoors, place them in a cool bag until needed.

☆ Make sure meats such as burgers, sausages and poultry are thoroughly cooked—there should be no trace of pink in the juices. Pierce a thick part of flesh as a test: the juices should run clear.

*RIGHT: Poultry can be precooked in the oven or microwave before being finished off on the grill*

*ABOVE: Light the fire with a long match or taper, and leave it to burn for about 15 minutes*

☆ Wash your hands after handling raw meat and before touching other foods. Don't use the same utensils for raw ingredients and cooked food.

☆ You may prefer to precook poultry in the microwave or oven and then transfer it to the grill to finish cooking and to attain the flavor of barbecued food. Don't allow meat to cool down before transferring it to the grill; poultry should never be reheated once it has already cooled.

☆ In case the fire should get out of control, have a bucket of sand and a water spray on hand to douse the flames.

☆ Keep a first-aid kit handy. If someone gets burnt, hold the burn under cold running water.

☆ Trim excess fat from meat and don't use too much oil in marinades. Fat can cause dangerous flare-ups if too much is allowed to drip onto the fuel.

☆ Use long-handled grilling tools, such as forks, tongs and brushes, for turning and basting food; keep some oven gloves nearby, preferably the extra-long type, to protect your hands.

☆ Always keep the raw foods to be cooked away from foods that are ready to eat, to prevent cross-contamination.

# BASIC TIMING GUIDE

° ° °

It is almost impossible to give precise timing guides for barbecuing, as there are so many factors to consider. The heat will depend on the type and size of the grill, the type of fuel used, the height of the rack above the fire and, of course, the weather. Cooking times will also be affected by the thickness and type of food, the quality of the meat, and where on the grill it is placed.

Bearing this in mind, the chart below provides only a rough guide to timing. Food should always be tested to make sure it is thoroughly cooked. The times given here are total cooking times, allowing for the food to be turned. Most foods need turning only once, but smaller items, such as kebabs and sausages, need to be turned more frequently to ensure even cooking. Foods wrapped in foil cook more slowly and will need longer on the grill.

| TYPE OF FOOD | WEIGHT/ THICKNESS | HEAT | TOTAL COOKING TIME |
|---|---|---|---|
| BEEF | | | |
| steaks | 1 inch | hot | rare: 5 minutes |
| | | | medium: 8 minutes |
| | | | well done: 12 minutes |
| burgers | ¾ inch | hot | 6–8 minutes |
| kebabs | 1 inch | hot | 5–8 minutes |
| roasts | 3½ pounds | spit | 2–3 hours |
| LAMB | | | |
| leg steaks | ¾ inch | medium | 10–15 minutes |
| chops | 1 inch | medium | 10–15 minutes |
| kebabs | 1 inch | medium | 6–15 minutes |
| butterfly leg | 3 inches | low | rare: 40–45 minutes |
| | | | well done: 1 hour |
| rolled shoulder | 3½ pounds | spit | 1¼–1½ hours |
| PORK | | | |
| chops | 1 inch | medium | 15–18 minutes |
| kebabs | 1 inch | medium | 12–15 minutes |
| spareribs | | medium | 30–40 minutes |
| sausages | thick | medium | 8–10 minutes |
| roasts | 3½ pounds | spit | 2–3 hours |

| TYPE OF FOOD | WEIGHT/ THICKNESS | HEAT | TOTAL COOKING TIME |
|---|---|---|---|
| CHICKEN | | | |
| whole | 3½ pounds | spit | 1–1¼ hours |
| quarters | | medium | 30–35 minutes |
| boneless breasts | | medium | 10–15 minutes |
| drumsticks | | medium | 25–30 minutes |
| kebabs | | medium | 6–10 minutes |
| poussin, whole | 1 pound | spit | 25–30 minutes |
| poussin, split | 1 pound | medium | 25–30 minutes |
| DUCKLING | | | |
| whole | 5 pounds | spit | 1–1½ hours |
| half | | medium | 35–45 minutes |
| breasts, boneless | | medium | 15–20 minutes |
| FISH | | | |
| large, whole | 5–10 pounds | low/ medium | allow 10 minutes per 1 inch thickness |
| small, whole | 1¼–2 pounds | hot/ medium | 12–20 minutes |
| sardines | | hot/ medium | 4–6 minutes |
| steaks or fillets | 1 inch | medium | 6–10 minutes |
| kebabs | 1 inch | medium | 5–8 minutes |
| large shrimp in shell | | medium | 6–8 minutes |
| large shrimp, shelled | | medium | 4–6 minutes |
| scallops/mussels in shell | | medium | until open |
| scallops/mussels, shelled, skewered | | medium | 5–8 minutes |
| half lobster | | low/ medium | 15–20 minutes |

# MARINATING

Marinades are used to add flavor and to moisten or tenderize foods, particularly meat. Marinades can be either savory or sweet and are as varied as you want to make them: spicy, fruity, fragrant or exotic. Certain classic combinations always work well with certain foods. Usually, it is best to choose oily marinades for dry foods, such as lean meat or white fish, and wine- or vinegar-based marinades for rich foods with a higher fat content. Most marinades don't contain salt, which can draw out the juices from meat. It's better to add salt just before, or after, cooking.

**1** Place the food for marinating in a wide, nonmetallic dish or bowl, preferably a dish that is large enough to allow the food to lie in a single layer.

**2** Mix together the ingredients for the marinade according to the recipe. The marinade can usually be prepared in advance and stored in a jar with a screw-top lid until needed.

**3** Pour the marinade over the food and turn the food to coat it evenly.

**4** Cover the dish or bowl with plastic wrap and chill in the refrigerator for anywhere from 30 minutes up to several hours or overnight, depending on the recipe. Turn the food over occasionally, and spoon the marinade over it to make sure it is well coated.

**5** Remove the food with a slotted spoon, or lift it out with tongs, and drain off and reserve the marinade. If necessary, allow the food to come to room temperature before cooking.

**6** Use the marinade for basting or brushing the food during cooking.

### Cook's Tip
The amount of marinade you will need depends on the amount of food. As a rough guide, about ⅔ cup is enough for about 1¼ pounds of food.

BELOW: *Marinating foods before cooking adds to the flavor and ensures the food is kept tender and moist*

### BASIC BARBECUE MARINADE
*This can be used for meat or fish.*

*1 garlic clove, crushed*
*3 tablespoons sunflower or olive oil*
*3 tablespoons dry sherry*
*1 tablespoon Worcestershire sauce*
*1 tablespoon dark soy sauce*
*freshly ground black pepper*

### RED WINE MARINADE
*This is good with red meats and game.*

*⅔ cup dry red wine*
*1 tablespoon olive oil*
*1 tablespoon red wine vinegar*
*2 garlic cloves, crushed*
*2 dried bay leaves, crumbled*
*freshly ground black pepper*

# Appetizers & Snacks

# SKEWERED LAMB WITH RED ONION SALSA

*A simple salsa makes a refreshing accompaniment to this summery dish—make sure you use a mild-flavored red onion that is fresh and crisp, and a tomato that is ripe and full of flavor.*

### INGREDIENTS

8 ounces lean lamb, cubed
½ teaspoon ground cumin
1 teaspoon ground paprika
1 tablespoon olive oil
salt and freshly ground black pepper

FOR THE SALSA
1 red onion, very thinly sliced
1 large tomato, seeded and chopped
1 tablespoon red wine vinegar
3 or 4 fresh basil or mint leaves, roughly torn
small mint leaves, to garnish

SERVES 4

**1** Place the lamb in a large bowl with the cumin, paprika and olive oil and season with plenty of salt and freshly ground black pepper. Toss well. Cover the bowl with plastic wrap and let sit in a cool place for several hours or in the refrigerator overnight, so that the lamb fully absorbs the spicy flavors.

**2** Spear the lamb cubes on four small skewers. If using wooden skewers, soak them first in cold water for at least 30 minutes to prevent them from burning when placed on the grill.

**3** To make the salsa, put the sliced onion, tomato, red wine vinegar and torn fresh basil or mint leaves in a small bowl and stir together until thoroughly blended. Season to taste with salt and garnish with mint.

**4** Cook the skewered lamb on a hot grill or under a hot broiler for 5–10 minutes, turning the skewers frequently, until the lamb is well browned but still slightly pink in the center. Serve hot, with the salsa.

# HERB POLENTA

* ° °

*Golden polenta made with fresh summer herbs and served with grilled tomatoes makes a tasty appetizer or light snack.*

## INGREDIENTS

*3 cups stock or water*
*1 teaspoon salt*
*1 cup polenta*
*2 tablespoons butter*
*5 tablespoons mixed chopped fresh parsley, chives and basil, plus extra to garnish*
*olive oil for brushing*
*4 large plum or beef tomatoes, halved*
*salt and freshly ground black pepper*

SERVES 4

**3** Remove from the heat and stir in the butter, chopped herbs and pepper.

**4** Lightly grease a wide pan or dish and pour the polenta into it, spreading it evenly. Set aside until cool and set.

**1** Prepare the polenta in advance: Place the stock or water in a saucepan, with the salt, and bring to a boil. Reduce the heat and stir in the polenta.

**2** Stir constantly over moderate heat for 5 minutes, until the polenta begins to thicken and come away from the sides of the saucepan.

**5** Turn out the polenta and cut into squares or stamp out rounds with a large cookie cutter. Brush with olive oil. Lightly brush the tomatoes with oil and sprinkle with salt and pepper. Cook the tomatoes and polenta on a medium-hot grill for about 5 minutes, turning once. Serve garnished with fresh herbs.

### Cook's Tip

Try using fresh basil or fresh chives alone, for a distinctive flavor.

# BRIE PARCELS WITH ALMONDS

• • •

*Creamy French Brie makes a sophisticated appetizer or light meal, wrapped in grape leaves and served hot with chunks of crusty bread.*

**2** Cut the Brie into four chunks and place each chunk on a grape leaf.

**3** Mix together the chives, ground almonds, peppercorns and olive oil, and place a spoonful on top of each piece of cheese. Sprinkle with sliced almonds.

**4** Fold the grape leaves over tightly to enclose the cheese completely. Brush the parcels with olive oil and cook on a hot grill for 3–4 minutes, until the cheese is hot and melting. Serve immediately.

### INGREDIENTS

4 large grape leaves, in brine
7-ounce piece Brie cheese
2 tablespoons chopped fresh chives
2 tablespoons ground almonds
1 teaspoon crushed black peppercorns
1 tablespoon olive oil, plus extra for brushing
sliced almonds

SERVES 4

**1** Rinse the grape leaves thoroughly under cold running water and dry them well. Spread the leaves out on a clean work surface or chopping board.

# SALMON WITH SPICY PESTO

*This is a great way to bone salmon steaks to give a solid piece of fish. The pesto is made with sunflower or pumpkin seeds and chilies rather than the classic basil and pine nuts.*

### INGREDIENTS

4 salmon steaks, about
8 ounces each
2 tablespoons sunflower oil
finely grated rind and juice
of 1 lime
salt and freshly ground
black pepper

FOR THE PESTO
6 mild fresh red chilies
2 garlic cloves
2 tablespoons sunflower or
pumpkin seeds
juice and finely grated rind
of 1 lime
5 tablespoons olive oil

SERVES 4

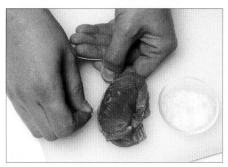

**1** Insert a very sharp knife close to the top of the bone. Working close to the bone, cut your way to the end of the steak to release one side. Repeat with the other side. Pull out any visible extra bones with a pair of tweezers.

**2** Sprinkle salt on a work surface and take hold of the end of the salmon piece, skin side down. Insert the knife between the skin and the flesh and, working away from you, remove the skin, keeping the knife as close to it as possible. Repeat for each piece of fish.

**3** Curl each piece of fish into a round, with the thinner end wrapped around the fatter end. Secure the shape tightly with a length of string.

**4** Rub the sunflower oil into the boneless fish rounds. Put the salmon in a large bowl or dish and add the lime juice and rind and the salt and pepper. Allow the salmon to marinate in the refrigerator for up to 2 hours.

**5** For the pesto, seed the chilies and place, with the garlic cloves, sunflower or pumpkin seeds, lime juice, rind and seasoning, in a food processor. Process until well mixed. With the blades moving, gradually pour in the olive oil until the sauce has thickened and emulsified. Drain the salmon from its marinade. Cook the fish steaks on a medium grill for 5 minutes on each side and serve with the spicy pesto.

# SPICY MEATBALLS

*These meatballs are delicious served piping hot with chili sauce. Keep the sauce on the side so that everyone can add as much heat as they like.*

### INGREDIENTS

*4 ounces fresh spicy sausages*
*4 ounces ground beef*
*2 shallots, finely chopped*
*2 garlic cloves, finely chopped*
*1½ cups fresh white bread crumbs*
*1 egg, beaten*
*2 tablespoons chopped fresh parsley, plus extra to garnish*
*1 tablespoon olive oil*
*salt and freshly ground black pepper*
*Tabasco or other hot chili sauce, to serve*

SERVES 6

**1** Use your hands to remove the skins from the sausages, placing the sausage meat in a mixing bowl and breaking it up with a fork.

**2** Add the ground beef, shallots, garlic, bread crumbs, beaten egg and parsley, with plenty of salt and pepper. Mix well, then use your hands to shape the mixture into 18 small balls.

**3** Brush the meatballs with olive oil and cook on a medium grill, or fry them in a large pan, for about 10–15 minutes, turning regularly until evenly browned and cooked through.

**4** Transfer the meatballs to a warm dish and sprinkle with chopped fresh parsley. Serve with chili sauce.

# POLPETTE WITH MOZZARELLA AND TOMATO

° ° °

*These Italian-style meatballs are made with beef and topped with creamy melted mozzarella and savory anchovies.*

## INGREDIENTS

*½ slice white bread, crusts removed*
*3 tablespoons milk*
*1½ pounds ground beef*
*1 egg, beaten*
*⅔ cup dry bread crumbs*
*olive oil for brushing*
*2 beefsteak or other large tomatoes, sliced*
*1 tablespoon chopped fresh oregano*
*6 slices mozzarella cheese*
*6 canned anchovy fillets, drained and cut in half lengthwise*
*salt and freshly ground black pepper*
SERVES 6

**1** Put the bread and milk into a small saucepan and heat very gently, until the bread absorbs all the milk. Mash it to a pulp and set aside to cool.

**2** Put the ground beef into a bowl with the bread mixture and the egg and season with plenty of salt and freshly ground black pepper. Mix well, then shape the mixture into 6 patties, using your hands. Sprinkle the bread crumbs onto a plate and dredge the patties, coating them thoroughly.

**3** Brush the polpette with olive oil and cook them on a hot grill for 2–3 minutes on one side, until brown. Turn them over.

**4** Without removing the polpette from the grill, lay a slice of tomato on top of each one, sprinkle with chopped oregano and season with salt and pepper. Place a mozzarella slice on top and arrange 2 strips of anchovy in a cross over the cheese.

**5** Cook for another 4–5 minutes, until the polpette are cooked through and the mozzarella has melted.

# FIVE-SPICE RIB-STICKERS

• • •

*To make these a real success, choose the meatiest spareribs you can find;
remember to keep a supply of paper napkins within easy reach.*

**2** Mix together all the remaining ingredients except the scallions; pour this mixture over the ribs. Toss well to coat evenly. Cover the bowl and let marinate in the refrigerator overnight.

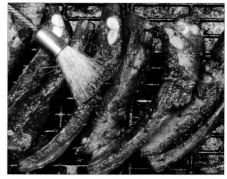

**3** Cook the ribs on a medium-hot grill, turning frequently, for 30–40 minutes. Brush occasionally with the remaining marinade.

### INGREDIENTS
2¼ pounds Chinese-style pork spareribs
2 teaspoons Chinese five-spice powder
2 garlic cloves, crushed
1 tablespoon grated fresh ginger
½ teaspoon chili sauce
4 tablespoons dark soy sauce
3 tablespoons dark brown sugar
1 tablespoon sunflower oil
4 scallions

SERVES 4

**1** If the spareribs are still attached to each other, cut between them to separate them (or you could ask your butcher to do this when you buy them). Place the spareribs in a large bowl.

**4** While the ribs are cooking, finely slice the scallions. Sprinkle them over the ribs and serve immediately.

# CHICKEN WINGS TERIYAKI STYLE

∘ ∘ ∘

*This Japanese-style glaze is very simple to prepare and adds a unique flavor to the meat.*
*The glaze can be used with any cut of chicken or with fish.*

### INGREDIENTS

1 garlic clove, crushed
3 tablespoons soy sauce
2 tablespoons dry sherry
2 teaspoons honey
2 teaspoons grated fresh ginger
1 teaspoon sesame oil
12 chicken wings
1 tablespoon sesame seeds, toasted

SERVES 4

**1** Place the garlic, soy sauce, sherry, honey, grated ginger and sesame oil in a large bowl and beat with a fork, to mix the ingredients together evenly.

**2** Add the chicken wings and toss thoroughly, to coat in the marinade. Cover the bowl with plastic wrap and chill for 30 minutes or longer.

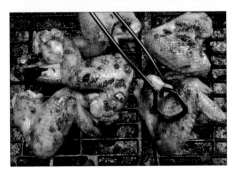

**3** Cook the chicken wings on a fairly hot grill for 20–25 minutes, turning occasionally and basting with the remaining marinade.

**4** Sprinkle the chicken wings with sesame seeds. Serve the wings on their own as an appetizer or side dish, or as a light meal with a crisp green salad.

# MEAT

~

# VEAL CHOPS WITH BASIL BUTTER

∘ ∘ ∘

*Veal chops from the loin are an expensive cut and are best cooked quickly and simply.*
*The flavor of basil goes well with veal, but other herbs can be used instead if you prefer.*

### INGREDIENTS

*2 tablespoons butter, softened*
*1 tablespoon Dijon mustard*
*1 tablespoon chopped fresh basil*
*olive oil, for brushing*
*2 veal loin chops, 1-inch thick,*
*8 ounces each*
*salt and freshly ground black*
*pepper*
*fresh basil sprigs, to garnish*

SERVES 2

**1** To make the basil butter, cream the softened butter with the Dijon mustard and chopped fresh basil in a large mixing bowl, then season with plenty of freshly ground black pepper.

**2** Brush both sides of each chop with olive oil and season with a little salt.

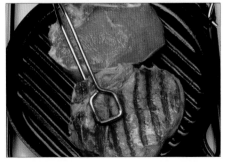

**3** Cook the chops on a hot grill for 7–10 minutes, basting with oil and turning once, until done to your liking. (Medium-rare meat will still be slightly soft when pressed, medium meat will be springy, and well-done firm.) Top each chop with half the basil butter and serve at once, garnished with basil.

# MIXED GRILL SKEWERS WITH HORSERADISH SAUCE

° ° °

*This hearty selection of meats, cooked on a skewer and drizzled with horseradish sauce, makes a popular main course. Keep all the pieces of meat about the same thickness so they cook evenly.*

### INGREDIENTS

4 small lamb noisettes, each
about 1 inch thick
4 lamb kidneys
4 slices lean bacon
8 cherry tomatoes
8 chipolata sausages
12–16 bay leaves
salt and freshly ground black
pepper

FOR THE HORSERADISH SAUCE
2 tablespoons horseradish relish
3 tablespoons melted butter

SERVES 4

**1** Trim any excess fat from the lamb noisettes with a sharp knife. Halve the kidneys and remove the cores, using kitchen scissors.

**2** Cut each bacon slice in half and wrap around the tomatoes and kidneys.

**3** Thread the lamb noisettes, bacon-wrapped kidneys and cherry tomatoes, chipolatas and bay leaves onto 4 long metal skewers. Set aside while you prepare the sauce.

**4** Mix the horseradish relish with the melted butter in a small bowl and stir until thoroughly mixed.

**5** Brush a little of the horseradish sauce over the meat and sprinkle with salt and freshly ground black pepper.

**6** Cook the skewers on a medium grill for 12 minutes, turning them occasionally, until the meat is golden brown and thoroughly cooked. Serve hot, drizzled with the remaining sauce.

# SAUSAGES WITH PRUNES AND BACON

· · ·

*Sausages are a perennial barbecue favorite, and this is a delicious and
unusual way to prepare them. Serve with crusty French bread or warmed ciabatta.*

**2** Spread the cut surface with the
mustard and then place 3 prunes in
each sausage, pressing them in firmly.

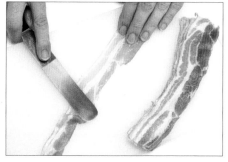

**3** Stretch the bacon slices out thinly,
using the back of a metal spatula.

**4** Wrap one bacon slice tightly
around each of the sausages, to
hold them in shape. Cook over a hot
grill for 15–18 minutes, turning
occasionally, until evenly browned and
thoroughly cooked. Serve at once, with
lots of fresh crusty bread and mustard.

### INGREDIENTS

*8 large garlic and herb pork
sausages, or other good-quality
meaty sausages
2 tablespoons Dijon mustard,
plus extra to serve
24 pitted prunes
8 slices lean smoked bacon*

SERVES 4

**1** Use a sharp knife to cut a long slit
down the length of each sausage, about
three-quarters of the way through.

# SHISH KEBAB

*Many different kinds of kebab are eaten throughout the Middle East, and they are
almost always cooked over an open wood or charcoal fire.*

### INGREDIENTS

1 pound boned leg of lamb, cubed
1 large green bell pepper, seeded
and cut into squares
1 large yellow bell pepper, seeded
and cut into squares
8 baby onions, halved
8 ounces button mushrooms
4 tomatoes, halved
1 tablespoons melted butter
bulgur, to serve

FOR THE MARINADE
3 tablespoons olive oil
juice of 1 lemon
2 garlic cloves, crushed
1 large onion, grated
1 tablespoon fresh oregano
salt and freshly ground black
pepper

SERVES 4

**1** First make the marinade: Blend
together the olive oil, lemon juice,
crushed garlic, onion, fresh oregano
and seasoning. Place the meat in
a shallow dish and pour the marinade
over it. Cover with plastic wrap and
allow to marinate for several hours,
or overnight, in the refrigerator.

**2** Thread the lamb onto metal
skewers, alternating with pieces of
pepper, onions and mushrooms. Thread
the tomatoes onto separate skewers.

**3** Cook the kebabs and tomatoes on
a hot grill for 10 minutes, turning
occasionally and basting with butter.
Serve with prepared bulgur.

# BACON KOFTA KEBABS AND SALAD

*Kofta kebabs can be made with any type of ground meat, but bacon is very successful, if you have a food processor.*

### INGREDIENTS

9 ounces lean bacon slices,
roughly chopped
1 small onion, roughly chopped
1 celery stick, roughly chopped
5 tablespoons fresh whole-wheat
bread crumbs
3 tablespoons chopped fresh thyme
2 tablespoons Worcestershire sauce
1 egg, beaten
salt and freshly ground black
pepper
olive oil, for brushing

FOR THE SALAD
3/4 cup bulgur wheat
4 tablespoons toasted sunflower
seeds
1 tablespoon olive oil
salt and freshly ground black
pepper
handful of celery leaves, chopped

SERVES 4

**1** Place the bacon, onion, celery and bread crumbs in a food processor and process until chopped. Add the thyme, Worcestershire sauce and seasoning. Bind to a firm mixture with the egg.

**2** Divide the mixture into 8 equal portions and use your hands to shape them around 8 bamboo skewers.

**3** For the salad, place the bulgur in a bowl and pour boiling water over it to cover. Let stand for 30 minutes, until the grains are tender.

**4** Drain well, then stir in the sunflower seeds, olive oil, salt and pepper. Stir in the celery leaves.

**5** Cook the kofta skewers over a medium-hot grill for 8–10 minutes, turning occasionally, until golden brown. Serve with the salad.

# PEPPERED STEAKS IN BEER AND GARLIC

*The robust flavors of this dish will satisfy the heartiest appetites.*
*Serve the steaks with baked potatoes and a crisp mixed salad.*

**2** Remove the steaks from the dish and reserve the marinade. Sprinkle the peppercorns over the steaks, and press them into the surface.

**3** Cook the steaks on a hot grill, basting them occasionally with the reserved marinade during cooking. (Take care when basting, as the alcohol will tend to flare up: Spoon or brush on just a small amount at a time.)

### INGREDIENTS

*4 beef sirloin or round steaks,*
*about 6 ounces each*
*2 garlic cloves, crushed*
*1/2 cup brown ale or stout*
*2 tablespoons dark brown sugar*
*2 tablespoons Worcestershire sauce*
*1 tablespoon corn oil*
*1 tablespoon crushed black*
*peppercorns*

SERVES 4

**1** Place the steaks in a dish and add the garlic, ale or stout, sugar, Worcestershire sauce and oil. Turn to coat evenly, then let marinate in the refrigerator for 2–3 hours or overnight.

**4** Turn the steaks once during cooking, and cook them for about 3–6 minutes on each side, depending on how rare you like them.

# SIRLOIN STEAKS WITH BLOODY MARY SAUCE

*This cocktail of ingredients is just as delicious as the drink that inspired it, and since the alcohol evaporates in cooking, it is perfectly safe to serve to children.*

### INGREDIENTS

*4 sirloin steaks, about 8 ounces each*

FOR THE MARINADE
*2 tablespoons dark soy sauce*
*4 tablespoons balsamic vinegar*
*2 tablespoons olive oil*

FOR THE BLOODY MARY SAUCE
*2¼ pounds very ripe tomatoes, peeled and chopped*
*tomato paste, if required*
*½ cup chopped onions*
*2 scallions*
*1 teaspoon chopped fresh cilantro*
*1 teaspoon ground cumin*
*1 teaspoon salt*
*1 tablespoon fresh lime juice*
*½ cup beef consommé*
*¼ cup vodka*
*1 tablespoon Worcestershire sauce*

SERVES 4

**1** Lay the steaks in a shallow dish. Mix the marinade ingredients together, pour over the steaks and let marinate in the refrigerator for at least 2 hours, turning once or twice.

**2** Place all the sauce ingredients in a food processor and blend to a fairly smooth texture. If the tomatoes are not quite ripe, add a little tomato paste. Put in a saucepan, bring to a boil and simmer for about 5 minutes.

**3** Remove the steaks from the dish and discard the marinade. Cook the steaks on a medium-hot grill for about 3–6 minutes on each side, depending on how rare you like them, turning once during cooking. Serve the steaks with the Bloody Mary Sauce.

# STILTON BURGERS

° ° °

*A variation on the traditional hamburger, this tasty recipe contains a delicious surprise:*
*a creamy filling of lightly melted Stilton cheese.*

### INGREDIENTS

1 pound ground beef
1 onion, chopped
1 celery stick, chopped
1 teaspoon dried mixed herbs
1 teaspoon prepared mustard
½ cup crumbled Stilton cheese
4 hamburger buns
salt and freshly ground black
pepper
salad and mustard pickle, to serve

SERVES 4

**1** Mix the ground beef with the chopped onion, celery, mixed herbs and mustard. Season well with salt and pepper, and bring together with your hands to form a firm mixture.

**2** Divide the mixture into 8 equal portions. Shape 4 portions into rounds and flatten each one slightly. Place a little of the crumbled cheese in the center of each round.

**3** Shape and flatten the remaining four portions and place on top. Use your hands to mold the rounds together, encasing the crumbled cheese and shaping them into four burgers.

**4** Cook on a medium grill for about 10 minutes or until cooked through, turning once. Split the hamburger buns and place a burger inside each one. Serve with salad and mustard pickle.

# SPICED BEEF SATAY

*Tender strips of steak threaded on skewers and spiced with the characteristic flavors of Indonesia are popular with everyone. Tamarind pulp can be found in Asian markets.*

### INGREDIENTS

1 pound sirloin steak, cut into
½-inch strips
1 teaspoon coriander seeds, dry-
fried and ground
½ teaspoon cumin seeds, dry-fried
and ground
1 teaspoon tamarind pulp
1 small onion
2 garlic cloves
1 tablespoon brown sugar
1 tablespoon dark soy sauce
salt

TO SERVE
cucumber chunks
lemon or lime wedges
Sambal Kecap

MAKES 18 SKEWERS

**1** Mix the meat and spices in a large nonmetallic bowl. Soak the tamarind pulp in ⅓ cup water.

**2** Strain the tamarind and reserve the juice. Put the onion, garlic, tamarind juice, sugar and soy sauce in a food processor and blend well.

**3** Pour the marinade over the meat and spices and toss together well. Let stand for at least 1 hour.

**4** Meanwhile, soak some bamboo skewers in water to prevent them from burning while cooking. Thread 5 or 6 pieces of meat onto each skewer and sprinkle with salt. Cook on a hot grill, turning frequently and basting with the marinade, until tender.

**5** Serve with cucumber chunks and wedges of lemon or lime for squeezing over the meat. Sambal Kecap is a traditional accompaniment.

SAMBAL KECAP
Mix 1 fresh red chili,
seeded and finely chopped,
2 crushed garlic cloves and
4 tablespoons dark soy sauce with
4 teaspoons lemon juice and
2 tablespoons hot water in a
bowl. Let stand for 30 minutes
before serving.

# LAMB STEAKS MARINATED IN MINT AND SHERRY

• • •

*The marinade in this recipe is extremely quick to prepare, and is the key
to its success: the sherry imparts a wonderful tang to the meat.*

## INGREDIENTS
6 large lamb steaks or
12 smaller chops

FOR THE MARINADE
2 tablespoons chopped fresh mint
leaves
1 tablespoons black peppercorns
1 medium onion, chopped
½ cup sherry
4 tablespoons extra virgin olive oil
2 garlic cloves

SERVES 6

**1** Finely chop the mint leaves and
peppercorns in a food processor. Add
the onion and process again until
smooth. Add the rest of the marinade
ingredients and process until
completely mixed. The marinade
should have a thick consistency.

**2** Add the marinade to the meat and
cover with plastic wrap. Place in the
refrigerator to marinate overnight.

**3** Cook the steaks on a medium grill
for 10–15 minutes, basting occasionally
with the marinade.

# SKEWERED LAMB WITH CILANTRO YOGURT

*These Turkish kebabs are traditionally made with lamb, but lean beef or pork works equally well.*
*You can alternate pieces of bell pepper, lemon or onions with the meat for extra flavor and color.*

### INGREDIENTS

2 pounds boneless lean lamb
1 large onion, grated
3 bay leaves
5 sprigs of thyme or rosemary
grated rind and juice of 1 lemon
1/2 teaspoon sugar
1/3 cup olive oil
salt and freshly ground black
pepper
sprigs of fresh rosemary, to garnish
barbecued lemon wedges, to serve

FOR THE CILANTRO YOGURT
2/3 cup thick plain yogurt
1 tablespoon chopped fresh mint
1 tablespoon chopped fresh
cilantro
2 teaspoons grated onion

SERVES 4

**1** To make the cilantro yogurt, mix together the yogurt, chopped fresh mint, chopped fresh cilantro and grated onion. Transfer the yogurt to a serving bowl.

**2** To make the kebabs, cut the lamb into 1-inch cubes and place in a bowl. Mix together the onion, herbs, lemon rind and juice, sugar and oil, then season to taste.

**3** Pour the marinade over the meat in the bowl and stir so that the meat is thoroughly covered. Cover with plastic wrap and marinate in the refrigerator for several hours or overnight.

**4** Drain the meat and thread onto metal skewers. Cook on a hot grill for about 10 minutes. Garnish with rosemary and grilled lemon wedges and serve with the cilantro yogurt.

# LAMB BURGERS WITH RED CURRANT CHUTNEY

*These very special burgers take a little extra time to prepare but are well worth it.
The red currant chutney is the perfect complement to the minty lamb taste.*

### INGREDIENTS

1¼ pounds ground lean lamb
1 small onion, finely chopped
2 tablespoons finely chopped
fresh mint
2 tablespoons finely chopped
fresh parsley
4 ounces mozzarella cheese
2 tablespoons oil, for basting
salt and freshly ground black
pepper

FOR THE RED CURRANT CHUTNEY
1½ cups fresh or frozen red
currants
2 teaspoons clear honey
1 teaspoon balsamic vinegar
2 tablespoons finely chopped mint

SERVES 4

**2** Roughly divide the meat mixture into eight equal pieces and use your hands to press each of the pieces into a flat round.

**3** Cut the mozzarella into 4 chunks. Place 1 chunk of cheese on half the lamb rounds. Top each one with another round of meat mixture.

**4** Press each of the 2 rounds of meat together firmly, making 4 flattish burger shapes. Use your fingers to blend the edges and seal in the cheese completely.

**5** Place all the ingredients for the chutney in a bowl and mash them together with a fork. Season well with salt and freshly ground black pepper.

**6** Brush the lamb burgers with olive oil and cook them on a moderately hot grill for about 15 minutes, turning once, until golden brown. Serve on hamburger buns with the chutney.

**1** In a large bowl, mix together the ground lamb, chopped onion, mint and parsley until evenly combined. Season well with plenty of salt and freshly ground black pepper.

### Cook's Tip

If time is short, or if fresh red currants are not available, serve the burgers with ready-made red currant sauce.

# PORK AND PINEAPPLE SATAY

. . .

*This variation on the classic Thai satay has added pineapple, but keeps the traditional coconut and peanut sauce.*

### INGREDIENTS

1¼ pound pork fillet
1 small onion, chopped
1 garlic clove, chopped
4 tablespoons soy sauce
finely grated rind of ½ lemon
1 teaspoon ground cumin
1 teaspoon ground cilantro
1 teaspoon ground turmeric
1 teaspoon dark brown sugar
1 8-ounce can pineapple chunks in
juice, or 1 small fresh pineapple,
peeled and diced
salt and freshly ground black
pepper

FOR THE SATAY SAUCE
¾ cup coconut milk
6 tablespoons crunchy peanut
butter
1 garlic clove, crushed
2 teaspoons soy sauce
1 teaspoon dark brown sugar

SERVES 4

**1** Using a sharp kitchen knife, trim any fat from the pork fillet and cut it into 1-inch cubes. Place the meat in a large mixing bowl and set aside.

**2** Place the onion, garlic, soy sauce, lemon rind, spices and sugar in a blender or food processor. Add two pieces of pineapple and process until the mixture is almost smooth.

**3** Add to the pork, tossing well to coat evenly. Thread pork onto bamboo skewers (soak skewers in water first), with the remaining pineapple pieces.

**4** To make the sauce, pour the coconut milk into a small saucepan and stir in the peanut butter. Stir in the remaining sauce ingredients and heat gently on the grill, stirring, until smooth and hot. Cover and keep warm on the edge of the grill.

**5** Cook the pork and pineapple skewers on a medium-hot grill for 10–12 minutes, turning occasionally, until golden brown and thoroughly cooked. Serve with the satay sauce.

### Cook's Tip
You can use creamed coconut, a solid available in blocks at Asian markets, to make the coconut milk. Dissolve a 2-ounce piece in ⅔ cup boiling water and use as above.

# LEMONGRASS PORK CHOPS WITH MUSHROOMS

*Thai flavorings are used to make an aromatic marinade and a spicy sauce. The sauce can be put together in a pan on the grill while the chops and mushrooms are cooking.*

## INGREDIENTS

4 pork chops, about 8 ounces each
4 large field mushrooms
3 tablespoons vegetable oil
4 fresh red chilies, seeded and
finely sliced
3 tablespoons Thai fish sauce
6 tablespoons lime juice
4 shallots, chopped
1 teaspoon roasted ground rice
2 tablespoons chopped scallions
fresh cilantro leaves,
to garnish
4 scallions, shredded,
to garnish

FOR THE MARINADE
2 garlic cloves, chopped
1 tablespoon sugar
1 tablespoon Thai fish sauce
2 tablespoons soy sauce
1 tablespoon sesame oil
1 tablespoon whiskey or dry sherry
2 stalks lemongrass, finely
chopped
2 scallions, chopped

SERVES 4

**2** Place the mushrooms and marinated pork chops on a rack and brush with 1 tablespoon vegetable oil. On a medium-hot grill, cook the pork chops for 10–15 minutes and the mushrooms for about 2 minutes, turning once. Brush both with the marinade while cooking.

**3** Meanwhile, heat the remaining oil in a small frying pan, then remove from the heat and mix in the remaining ingredients. Put the pork chops and mushrooms on a serving plate and spoon the sauce over them. Garnish with the fresh cilantro leaves and shredded scallions.

**1** To make the marinade, mix all the ingredients. Arrange the pork chops in a shallow dish. Pour the marinade over them and let sit for 1–2 hours.

# STUFFED ROAST LOIN OF PORK

° ° °

*This recipe uses fruit and nuts as a stuffing for roast pork in the Catalan style. It is full of flavor and is very good served cold, making an excellent centerpiece for a summer buffet or a picnic.*

## INGREDIENTS

4 tablespoons olive oil
1 onion, finely chopped
2 garlic cloves, chopped
1 cup fresh bread crumbs
4 dried figs, chopped
8 pitted green olives, chopped
¼ cup sliced almonds
1 tablespoon lemon juice
1 tablespoon chopped fresh parsley
1 egg yolk
2-pound boned loin of pork
salt and freshly ground black
pepper

SERVES 4

**1** Preheat the oven to 400°F, or prepare the grill. Heat 3 tablespoons of the oil in a pan, add the onion and garlic, and cook gently until softened. Remove the pan from the heat and stir in the bread crumbs, figs, olives, almonds, lemon juice, chopped fresh parsley and egg yolk. Season to taste with salt and ground black pepper.

**2** Remove any string from the pork and unroll the belly flap, cutting away any excess fat or meat to enable you to do so. Spread the stuffing over the flat piece and roll it up, starting from the thick side. Tie at intervals with string.

**3** Pour the remaining olive oil into a roasting pan and put in the pork, or arrange on the spit of the grill. Roast for 1 hour and 15 minutes, or until the juices from the meat run clear.

**4** Remove the pork from the oven or the spit and, if serving hot, let it rest for 10 minutes before carving into thick slices. If serving cold, wrap the meat in foil to keep it moist until you carve it.

# POULTRY

~

# GRILLED CASHEW CHICKEN

*This dish comes from the beautiful Indonesian island of Bali, where nuts are widely used as a base for sauces and marinades. Serve it with a green salad and a hot chili dipping sauce.*

## INGREDIENTS

4 chicken legs
radishes, sliced, to garnish
1/2 cucumber, sliced, to garnish
Chinese cabbage, to serve

### FOR THE MARINADE
2 ounces raw cashew or
macadamia nuts
2 shallots, or 1 small onion, finely
chopped
2 garlic cloves, crushed
2 small red chilies, chopped
2-inch piece lemongrass
1 tablespoon tamarind sauce
2 tablespoons dark soy sauce
1 tablespoon Thai fish sauce
2 teaspoons sugar
1/2 teaspoon salt
1 tablespoon rice or white wine
vinegar

### SERVES 4

**1** Using a sharp kitchen knife, slash the chicken legs several times through to the bone. Chop off the knuckle end and discard.

**2** To make the marinade, place the cashew or macadamia nuts in a food processor and grind until fine (or use a pestle and mortar to grind them).

**3** Add the chopped shallots or onion, garlic, chilies and lemongrass and blend. Add the remaining marinade ingredients and blend again.

**4** Spread the marinade over the chicken and leave for up to 8 hours in the refrigerator. Cook the chicken on a medium grill for 25 minutes, basting and turning occasionally. Garnish with radishes and cucumber and serve on a bed of Chinese cabbage.

# CITRUS KEBABS

· · ·

*Serve these succulent grilled chicken kebabs on a bed of lettuce leaves, garnished with sprigs of fresh mint and orange and lemon slices.*

### INGREDIENTS

4 chicken breasts, skinned and
boned
fresh mint sprigs, to garnish
orange, lemon or lime slices, to
garnish

FOR THE MARINADE
finely grated rind and juice of
1/2 orange
finely grated rind and juice of
1/2 lemon or lime
2 tablespoons olive oil
2 tablespoons clear honey
2 tablespoons chopped fresh mint
1/4 teaspoon ground cumin
salt and freshly ground black
pepper

SERVES 4

**1** Use a heavy knife to cut the chicken into 1-inch cubes.

**2** Mix the marinade ingredients together in a large mixing bowl, add the chicken and cover with plastic wrap. Allow to marinate for at least 2 hours, or overnight in the refrigerator.

**3** Thread the chicken onto metal skewers and cook on a medium grill for 10 minutes, basting with the marinade and turning frequently. Garnish with mint and citrus slices.

# SWEET AND SOUR KEBABS

. . .

*This marinade contains sugar and will burn very easily, so cook the kebabs slowly
and turn them often. Serve these kebabs with Harlequin Rice.*

### INGREDIENTS

2 chicken breasts, skinned and
boned
8 pearl onions or 2 medium
onions
4 slices lean bacon
3 firm bananas
1 red bell pepper, diced

FOR THE MARINADE
2 tablespoons brown sugar
1 tablespoon Worcestershire sauce
2 tablespoons lemon juice
salt and freshly ground black
pepper

FOR THE HARLEQUIN RICE
2 tablespoons olive oil
1 small red bell pepper, diced
generous 1 cup cooked rice
1 cup cooked peas

SERVES 4

**1** Mix together the marinade ingredients. Cut each chicken breast into four pieces, add to the marinade, cover and leave for at least 4 hours, or preferably overnight in the refrigerator.

**2** Peel the pearl onions, blanch them in boiling water for 5 minutes and drain. If using medium onions, quarter them after blanching.

**3** Cut each slice of bacon in half with a sharp knife. Peel the bananas and cut each one into three pieces. Wrap half a bacon rasher around each of the banana pieces.

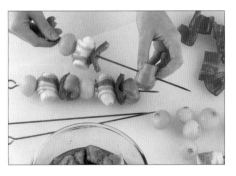

**4** Thread the bacon and bananas onto metal skewers with the chicken pieces, onions and pepper pieces. Brush generously with the marinade.

**5** Cook on a low grill for about 15 minutes, turning and basting frequently with the marinade.

**6** Meanwhile, heat the oil in a frying pan and stir-fry the diced pepper briefly. Add the rice and peas and stir until heated through. Serve Harlequin Rice with the kebabs.

# BLACKENED CAJUN CHICKEN AND CORN

* * *

*This is a classic Deep South method of cooking in a spiced coating, which can be used for poultry, meat or fish. The coating should begin to char and blacken slightly at the edges.*

### INGREDIENTS

8 chicken joints (drumsticks, thighs or wings)
2 ears of fresh corn
2 teaspoons garlic salt
2 teaspoons ground black pepper
1½ teaspoons ground cumin
1½ teaspoons paprika
1 teaspoon cayenne pepper
3 tablespoons melted butter
chopped parsley, to garnish

SERVES 4

**1** Trim any excess fat from the chicken, but leave the skin in place. Slash the thickest parts with a knife, to allow the flavors to penetrate the meat as much as possible.

**2** Pull the husks and silks off the ears of corn, then rinse them under cold running water and pat them dry with paper towels. Cut into thick slices, using a heavy kitchen knife.

**3** Mix together all the spices. Brush the chicken and corn with the melted butter and sprinkle the spices over them. Toss well to coat evenly.

**4** Cook the chicken pieces on a medium-hot grill for about 25 minutes, turning occasionally. Add the corn after 15 minutes and grill, turning often, until golden brown. Serve garnished with chopped parsley.

# CHICKEN WITH HERB AND RICOTTA STUFFING

*These little chicken drumsticks are full of flavor, and the stuffing and bacon help to keep them moist and tender.*

### INGREDIENTS

4 tablespoons ricotta cheese
1 garlic clove, crushed
3 tablespoons mixed chopped fresh herbs, such as chives, flat-leaf parsley and mint
2 tablespoons fresh brown bread crumbs
8 chicken drumsticks
8 slices lean smoked bacon
1 teaspoon whole-grain mustard
1 tablespoon sunflower oil
salt and freshly ground black pepper

SERVES 4

**1** Mix together the ricotta, garlic, herbs and bread crumbs. Season well with plenty of salt and pepper.

**2** Carefully loosen the skin from each drumstick and spoon a little of the herb stuffing underneath, smoothing the skin back over firmly.

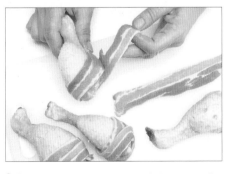

**3** Wrap a bacon slice tightly around the wide end of each drumstick, to hold the skin in place over the stuffing during cooking.

**4** Mix together the mustard and oil and brush them over the chicken. Cook on a medium-hot grill for about 25 minutes, turning occasionally.

# BABY CHICKENS WITH LIME AND CHILI

*Poussins are small birds that are ideal for one to two portions. The best way to prepare them is spatchcocked—split and flattened out—to ensure more even cooking.*

## INGREDIENTS

*4 poussins or Cornish game hens, about 1 pound each*
*3 tablespoons butter*
*2 tablespoons sun-dried tomato paste*
*finely grated rind of 1 lime*
*2 teaspoons chili sauce*
*juice of ½ lime*
*lime wedges, to serve*
*fresh flat leaf parsley sprigs, to garnish*

SERVES 4

**1** Place each poussin or hen on a chopping board, breast side upward, and press down firmly with your hand, to break the breastbone.

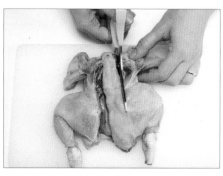

**2** Turn the poussin over and, with poultry shears or strong kitchen scissors, cut down either side of the backbone. Remove it and discard.

**3** Turn the poussin breast side up and flatten it gently. Lift the breast skin carefully and gently ease your fingertips underneath, to loosen it from the flesh.

**4** Mix together the butter, sun-dried tomato paste, lime rind and chili sauce in a small bowl. Spread about three-quarters of the mixture under the skin of the poussins, smoothing it evenly over the surface of the flesh.

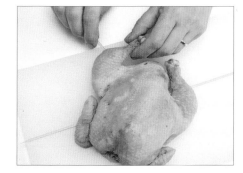

**5** To hold the poussins flat during cooking, thread two skewers through each bird, crossing at the center. Each skewer should pass through a drumstick and then out through a wing on the other side.

**6** Mix the reserved paste with the lime juice and brush it over the skin of the poussins. Cook on a medium-hot grill, turning occasionally, for 25–30 minutes, or until there is no trace of pink in the juices when the flesh is pierced. Garnish with lime wedges and fresh flat leaf parsley.

# Thai Grilled Chicken

. . .

*Thai grilled chicken is especially delicious when cooked outdoors on the barbecue.*
*Serve it on a bed of crisp salad with lime wedges to offset its richness.*

### INGREDIENTS

2 pounds chicken drumsticks or
thighs
salt and freshly ground
black pepper
crisp lettuce leaves, to serve
1/2 cucumber, cut into strips,
to garnish
4 scallions, trimmed,
to garnish
2 limes, quartered, to garnish

FOR THE MARINADE
1 teaspoon black peppercorns
1/2 teaspoon caraway or cumin
seeds
4 teaspoons sugar
2 teaspoons paprika
3/4-inch piece fresh ginger, chopped
3 garlic cloves, crushed
1 tablespoon finely chopped fresh
cilantro, white root or stem
3 tablespoons vegetable oil

SERVES 4–6

**1** Chop through the narrow end of each drumstick with a heavy knife. Score the chicken pieces deeply to allow the marinade to penetrate and arrange in a shallow bowl.

**2** Grind the peppercorns, caraway or cumin seeds and sugar with a mortar and pestle or in a food processor. Add the paprika, ginger, garlic, cilantro and oil and grind to a paste.

**3** Spread the marinade over the chicken and let marinate in the refrigerator for 6 hours. Cook the chicken on a medium grill for about 20 minutes, basting with the marinade and turning once. Season, arrange on a bed of lettuce and garnish before serving.

# MEDITERRANEAN TURKEY SKEWERS

*These attractive kebabs can be assembled in advance and left to marinate until you are ready to cook them. Grilling intensifies the Mediterranean flavors of the vegetables.*

### INGREDIENTS

2 medium zucchini
1 long thin eggplant
11 ounces boneless turkey, cut
into 2-inch cubes
12–16 pearl onions
1 red or yellow bell pepper, cut
into 2-inch squares

FOR THE MARINADE
6 tablespoons olive oil
3 tablespoons fresh lemon juice
1 garlic clove, finely chopped
2 tablespoons chopped fresh basil
salt and freshly ground black
pepper

SERVES 4

**3** Prepare the skewers by alternating the turkey, onions and pepper pieces. Lay the prepared skewers on a platter and sprinkle with the flavored oil. Allow to marinate for 30 minutes.

**4** Cook on a medium grill or under a broiler, turning the skewers occasionally, for about 10 minutes, or until the turkey is cooked and the vegetables are tender.

**1** To make the marinade, mix the olive oil with the lemon juice, garlic and chopped fresh basil. Season well with plenty of salt and black pepper.

**2** Slice the zucchini and eggplant lengthwise into strips ¼ inch thick. Cut them crosswise about two-thirds down their length. Discard the shorter lengths. Wrap half the turkey pieces with the zucchini slices and the other half with the eggplant slices.

# QUAIL WITH A FIVE-SPICE MARINADE

• • •

*Blending and grinding your own five-spice powder for this Vietnamese dish will give the freshest-tasting results. If you are short of time, buy a ready-mixed blend from the supermarket.*

### INGREDIENTS

*6 quail, cleaned*
*2 scallions, roughly chopped,*
*to garnish*
*mandarin orange or satsuma,*
*to garnish*
*banana leaves, to serve*

##### FOR THE MARINADE
*2 pieces star anise*
*2 teaspoons ground cinnamon*
*2 teaspoons fennel seeds*
*2 teaspoons Sichuan pepper*
*a pinch ground cloves*
*1 small onion, finely chopped*
*1 garlic clove, crushed*
*4 tablespoons clear honey*
*2 tablespoons dark soy sauce*

##### SERVES 4–6

**1** Remove the backbones from the quail by cutting down each side with a pair of strong kitchen scissors.

**2** Flatten the birds with the palm of your hand and secure each bird using two bamboo skewers.

**3** To make the marinade, place the five spices in a spice mill and grind into a fine powder (or grind using a mortar and pestle). Add the chopped onion, garlic, clear honey and soy sauce, and combine until thoroughly mixed.

**4** Arrange the quail on a flat dish and pour the marinade over them. Cover the dish with plastic wrap and let the quail marinate in the refrigerator for 8 hours or overnight.

**5** Cook the quail on a medium grill for 15–20 minutes, until golden brown, basting occasionally with the marinade and turning once.

**6** To garnish, remove the outer zest from the mandarin orange or satsuma, using a vegetable peeler. Shred the zest finely and combine with the chopped scallions. Arrange the quail on a bed of banana leaves and garnish with the orange zest and scallions.

#### Cook's Tip
If you prefer, or if quail are not available, you could use other poultry, such as poussins or Cornish game hens, as a substitute.

# DUCK BREASTS WITH RED PLUMS

. . .

*The rich fruity sauce for this dish combines brandy and red plums with heavy cream and cilantro. The sauce can be made in a pan on the grill while the duck is cooking.*

## INGREDIENTS

*4 duck breasts, about 6 ounces
each, skinned*
*2 teaspoons crushed cinnamon stick*
*4 tablespoons butter*
*1 tablespoon plum brandy or
cognac*
*1 cup chicken stock*
*1 cup heavy cream*
*6 fresh red plums, pitted and sliced*
*6 sprigs fresh cilantro leaves, plus
extra to garnish*
*salt and freshly ground black
pepper*

SERVES 4

**1** Score the duck breasts and sprinkle with salt. Press the crushed cinnamon onto both sides of the duck breasts. Brush with butter and cook on a medium grill for 15–20 minutes, turning once, until the duck is tender.

**2** To make the sauce, melt half the remaining butter in a saucepan. Add the brandy or cognac and set it alight. When the flames have died down, add the stock and cream and allow to simmer gently until reduced and thickened. Add seasoning to taste.

**3** In a saucepan, melt the other half of the butter and fry the plums with the cilantro just enough to cook the fruit through. Slice the duck breasts and pour some sauce around each one, then garnish with the plum slices and the chopped fresh cilantro.

# DUCK BREASTS WITH RED PEPPER JELLY GLAZE

*Sweet potatoes have pinkish skins and flesh varying from creamy white to deep orange.*
*Choose a long, cylindrical tuber to make neat round slices for this Cajun dish.*

## INGREDIENTS

*2 duck breasts*
*1 sweet potato, about 14 ounces*
*2 tablespoons red pepper jelly*
*1 tablespoon sherry vinegar*
*4 tablespoons butter, melted*
*coarse sea salt and freshly ground*
*black pepper*

SERVES **2**

**4** Meanwhile, warm the red pepper jelly and sherry vinegar together in a bowl set over a saucepan of hot water, stirring to mix them as the jelly melts. Brush the skin of the duck with this jelly glaze and return to the grill, skin side down, for another 2–3 minutes to caramelize it.

**5** Brush the sweet potato slices with melted butter and sprinkle with coarse sea salt. Cook on a hot grill for 8–10 minutes, until soft, brushing with more butter and sprinkling with salt and pepper when you turn them. Serve the duck sliced with the sweet potatoes and accompany with a green salad.

**1** Slash the skin of the duck breasts diagonally at 1-inch intervals and rub plenty of salt and pepper over the skin and into the cuts.

**2** Scrub the sweet potato and cut into ½-inch slices, discarding the ends.

**3** Cook the duck breasts on a medium grill, skin side down, for 5 minutes. Turn and cook for another 8–10 minutes, according to how pink you like your duck.

# FISH &
# SHELLFISH

~

# JUMBO SHRIMP SKEWERS WITH WALNUT PESTO

*This is an unusual appetizer or main course, which can be prepared in advance and kept in the refrigerator until you're ready to cook it.*

### INGREDIENTS

12–16 raw, unshelled jumbo shrimp
½ cup walnut pieces
4 tablespoons chopped fresh
flat-leaf parsley
4 tablespoons chopped fresh basil
2 garlic cloves, chopped
3 tablespoons grated fresh
Parmesan cheese
2 tablespoons extra virgin olive oil
2 tablespoons walnut oil
salt and freshly ground black
pepper

SERVES 4

**3** Add half the pesto to the shrimp in the bowl, toss them well, then cover and chill in the refrigerator for a minimum of 1 hour, or overnight.

**4** Thread the shrimp onto skewers and cook them on a hot grill for 3–4 minutes, turning once. Serve with the remaining pesto and a green salad.

**1** Peel the shrimp, removing the heads but leaving the tails. Devein and then put the shrimp in a large mixing bowl.

**2** To make the pesto, place the walnuts, parsley, basil, garlic, cheese and oils in a food processor and process until finely chopped. Season.

# SWORDFISH KEBABS

. . .

*Swordfish has a firm, meaty texture that makes it ideal for cooking on the grill. Marinate the fish first to keep it moist.*

### INGREDIENTS

*2 pounds swordfish steaks*
*3 tablespoons olive oil*
*juice of ½ lemon*
*1 garlic clove, crushed*
*1 teaspoon paprika*
*3 tomatoes, quartered*
*2 onions, cut into wedges*
*salt and freshly ground black pepper*
*salad and pita bread, to serve*

SERVES 4–6

**1** Use a large kitchen knife to cut the swordfish steaks into large cubes. Arrange the cubes in a single layer in a large shallow dish.

**2** Blend together the olive oil, lemon juice, garlic, paprika and seasoning in a bowl, and pour the mixture over the fish. Cover the dish loosely with plastic wrap and allow to marinate in a cool place for up to 2 hours.

**3** Thread the fish cubes onto metal skewers, alternating them with the pieces of tomato and onion wedges.

**4** Cook the kebabs on a hot grill for 5–10 minutes, basting frequently with the remaining marinade and turning occasionally. Serve with salad and pita bread.

60

# CALAMARI WITH TWO-TOMATO STUFFING

· · ·

*Calamari, or baby squid, cook very quickly; be sure to turn and baste them often
and take care not to overcook them.*

### INGREDIENTS

1¼ pounds baby squid, cleaned
1 garlic clove, crushed
3 plum tomatoes, skinned and
chopped
8 sun-dried tomatoes in oil,
drained and chopped
4 tablespoons chopped fresh basil,
plus extra, to serve
4 tablespoons fresh white bread
crumbs
3 tablespoons olive oil
1 tablespoon red wine vinegar
salt and freshly ground black
pepper
lemon juice, to serve

SERVES 4

**1** Remove the tentacles from the
squid and roughly chop them; leave
the main part of the squid whole.

**2** Mix together the crushed garlic,
plum tomatoes, sun-dried tomatoes,
chopped fresh basil and bread crumbs.
Stir in 1 tablespoon of the olive oil and
the vinegar. Season with plenty of salt
and freshly ground black pepper. Soak
some wooden toothpicks in water for
10 minutes before use, to prevent them
from burning on the grill.

**3** Using a teaspoon, fill the squid
with the stuffing mixture. Secure the
open ends with the toothpicks to hold
the stuffing mixture in place.

**4** Brush the squid with the remaining
olive oil and cook over a medium-hot
grill for 4–5 minutes, turning often.
Sprinkle with lemon juice and extra
chopped fresh basil to serve.

# GRILLED SCALLOPS WITH LIME BUTTER

*Fresh scallops cook quickly, so they're ideal for barbecues. This recipe combines them simply with lime and fennel.*

### INGREDIENTS

1 fennel bulb
2 limes
12 large scallops, cleaned
1 egg yolk
6 tablespoons melted butter
olive oil for brushing
salt and freshly ground
black pepper

SERVES 4

**3** Place the egg yolk and remaining lime rind and juice in a small bowl and whisk until pale and smooth.

**5** Brush the fennel wedges with olive oil and cook them on a hot grill for 3–4 minutes, turning once.

**1** Trim any feathery leaves from the fennel and reserve them. Slice the bulb lengthwise into thin wedges.

**4** Gradually whisk in the melted butter and continue whisking until thick and smooth. Finely chop the reserved fennel leaves and stir them in, with seasoning to taste.

**6** Add the scallops and cook for another 3–4 minutes, turning once. Serve with the lime and fennel butter and the lime wedges.

**2** Cut one lime into wedges. Finely grate the rind and squeeze the juice from the other lime; toss half the juice and rind with the scallops. Season well with salt and fresh black pepper.

### Cook's Tip
If the scallops are small, you may wish to thread them onto flat skewers to make turning them easier.

# TROUT WITH BACON

· · ·

*The smoky, savory flavor of crisp grilled bacon perfectly complements*
*the delicate flesh of the trout in this simple dish.*

## INGREDIENTS

*4 trout, cleaned and gutted*
*1 tablespoon all-purpose flour*
*4 slices lean smoked bacon*
*2 tablespoons olive oil*
*juice of ¹/₂ lemon*
*salt and freshly ground*
*black pepper*

SERVES 4

**1** Place the trout on a chopping board and pat dry with paper towels. Season the flour with the salt and freshly ground black pepper. Stretch the bacon slices out thinly using the back of a heavy kitchen knife.

**2** Roll the fish in the seasoned flour mixture and wrap tightly in the bacon slices. Brush with olive oil and cook on a medium-hot grill for 10–15 minutes, turning once. Serve at once, with the lemon juice drizzled on top.

# Sardines with Warm Herb Salsa

*Plain grilling is the very best way to cook fresh sardines. Served with this luscious herb salsa, the only other essential item is fresh, crusty bread, to mop up the tasty juices.*

### INGREDIENTS

12–16 fresh sardines
oil, for brushing
juice of 1 lemon

FOR THE SALSA
1 tablespoon butter
4 scallions, chopped
1 garlic clove, finely chopped
rind of 1 lemon
2 tablespoons finely chopped
fresh parsley
2 tablespoons finely snipped
fresh chives
2 tablespoons finely chopped
fresh basil
2 tablespoon green olive paste
2 teaspoons balsamic vinegar
salt and freshly ground black
pepper

SERVES 4

**1** To clean the sardines, use a pair of small kitchen scissors to slit the fish along the belly and pull out the intestines. Wipe the fish with paper towels and then arrange on a grill rack.

**2** To make the salsa, melt the butter in a small pan and gently sauté the scallions and garlic for about 2 minutes, shaking the pan occasionally, until softened but not browned.

**3** Add the lemon rind and remaining salsa ingredients to the scallions and garlic in the pan and keep warm on the edge of the grill, stirring occasionally. Do not allow to boil.

**4** Brush the sardines lightly with oil and sprinkle with lemon juice, salt and pepper. Cook for about 2 minutes on each side, over moderate heat. Serve with the warm salsa and crusty bread.

# MONKFISH WITH PEPPERED CITRUS MARINADE

*. . .*

*Monkfish is a firm, meaty fish that keeps its shape well when cooked on the grill.*
*Serve with a green salad.*

### INGREDIENTS

*2 monkfish tails, about*
*12 ounces each*
*1 lime*
*1 lemon*
*2 oranges*
*handful of fresh thyme sprigs*
*2 tablespoons olive oil*
*1 tablespoon mixed peppercorns,*
*roughly crushed*
*salt and freshly ground*
*black pepper*

SERVES 4

**2** Turn the fish and repeat on the other side, to remove the second fillet. Repeat on the second tail. (If you prefer, you can ask your fishmonger to do this for you.) Lay the 4 fillets out flat on a chopping board.

**5** Squeeze the juice from the citrus fruits and mix it with the olive oil and more salt and pepper. Spoon over the fish. Cover with plastic wrap and marinate in the refrigerator for about 1 hour, turning occasionally and spooning the marinade over the fish.

**1** Using a sharp kitchen knife, remove any skin from the monkfish tails. Cut carefully down one side of the backbone, sliding the knife between the bone and the flesh, to remove the fillet on one side.

**3** Cut two slices from each of the citrus fruits and arrange them over 2 of the fillets. Add a few sprigs of fresh thyme and sprinkle with plenty of salt and freshly ground black pepper. Finely grate the rind from the remaining fruit and sprinkle it over the fish.

**6** Drain the monkfish, reserving the marinade, and sprinkle with the crushed peppercorns. Cook on a medium-hot grill for 15–20 minutes, basting with the marinade and turning occasionally, until the fish is evenly cooked. Serve immediately.

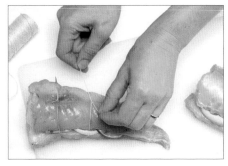

**4** Lay the other 2 fillets on top and tie them firmly at intervals.

# CHARBROILED TUNA WITH FIERY PEPPER PUREE

• • •

*Tuna is an oily fish that grills well and is meaty enough to combine successfully with strong*
*flavors—even hot chili, as in this red pepper purée, which is excellent served with crusty bread.*

### INGREDIENTS

4 tuna steaks, about 6 ounces each
finely grated rind and juice of 1 lime
2 tablespoons olive oil
salt and freshly ground black pepper
lime wedges and crusty bread, to serve

FOR THE PEPPER PURÉE
2 red bell peppers, halved
3 tablespoons olive oil, plus extra
for brushing
1 small onion
2 garlic cloves, crushed
2 fresh red chilies
1 slice white bread without crusts,
diced
salt

SERVES 4

**2** To make the pepper purée, brush the pepper halves with a little olive oil and cook them, skin side down, on a hot grill, until the skin is charred and blackened. Place the onion in its skin on the grill and cook until browned, turning it occasionally.

**4** Place the cooked peppers and onion with the garlic, chilies, bread and olive oil in a food processor. Process until smooth. Add salt to taste.

**3** Set aside the peppers and onion until cool enough to handle, then remove the skins, using a sharp knife.

**5** Drain the tuna steaks from the marinade and cook them on a hot grill for 8–10 minutes, turning once, until golden brown. Serve the steaks with the pepper purée and lime wedges, and crusty bread if desired.

**1** Trim any skin from the tuna and place the steaks in a single layer in a wide dish. Sprinkle with the lime rind and juice, olive oil, salt and black pepper. Cover with plastic wrap and chill in the refrigerator until needed.

### Cook's Tip

The pepper purée can be made ahead: cook the peppers and onion under a hot broiler and refrigerate them until you cook the fish.

# GRILLED SEA BASS WITH CITRUS FRUIT

• • •

*Sea bass is a beautiful fish with a soft, dense texture and a delicate flavor. In this recipe
it is complemented by citrus fruits and fruity olive oil.*

## INGREDIENTS

*1 small grapefruit*
*1 orange*
*1 lemon*
*1 sea bass, 3–3½ pounds, cleaned
and scaled*
*6 fresh basil sprigs*
*1 tablespoon olive oil, plus extra
for brushing*
*4–6 shallots, halved*
*4 tablespoons dry white wine*
*1 tablespoon butter*
*salt and freshly ground black
pepper*
*fresh dill, to garnish*

SERVES 6

**1** Using a vegetable peeler, remove the rind from the grapefruit, orange and lemon. Cut into thin julienne strips. Peel the pith from the fruits and, working over a bowl to catch the juices, cut out the segments from the grapefruit and the orange and set aside for the garnish. Slice the lemon thickly.

**2** Season the cavity of the fish with salt and pepper and slash the flesh 3 times on each side. Reserving a few basil sprigs for the garnish, fill the cavity with the remaining basil, the lemon slices and half the julienne strips of citrus rind. Brush with olive oil and cook on a medium-low grill for about 20 minutes, basting occasionally and turning once.

**3** Meanwhile, heat 1 tablespoon olive oil in a pan and cook the shallots gently until soft. Add the wine and 2–3 tablespoons of the fruit juice to the pan. Bring to a boil over high heat, stirring. Stir in the remaining julienne strips of rind and boil for 2–3 minutes, then whisk in the butter.

**4** When the fish is cooked, transfer it to a serving dish. Remove and discard the stuffing. Spoon the shallots and sauce around the fish and garnish with fresh dill sprigs, the reserved basil and segments of grapefruit and orange.

# SEA BREAM WITH ORANGE BUTTER SAUCE

∘ ∘ ∘

*Sea bream is a revelation to anyone unfamiliar with its creamy rich flavor.*
*The fish has a firm white flesh that goes well with this rich butter sauce, sharpened with orange.*

### INGREDIENTS

2 sea bream, about 12 ounces each,
scaled and gutted
2 teaspoons Dijon mustard
1 teaspoon fennel seeds
2 tablespoons olive oil, plus extra
for brushing
2 ounces watercress
6 ounces mixed lettuce leaves

### FOR THE ORANGE BUTTER SAUCE

2 tablespoons frozen orange juice
concentrate
12 tablespoons (1½ sticks) unsalted
butter, diced
salt and cayenne pepper

SERVES 2

**1** Slash the fish 4 times on each side. Combine the mustard and fennel seeds, then spread on both sides of the fish. Brush with olive oil and cook on a medium-hot grill for 10–12 minutes, turning once.

**2** Place the orange juice concentrate in a bowl and heat over a saucepan of simmering water. Remove the pan from the heat and gradually whisk in the butter until creamy. Season well.

**3** Dress the watercress and lettuce leaves with the remaining olive oil, and arrange with the fish on two plates. Spoon the sauce over the fish and serve with baked potatoes, if desired.

# MACKEREL KEBABS WITH SWEET PEPPER SALAD

*Mackerel is an excellent fish for grilling because its natural oils keep it moist and tasty.
This recipe combines mackerel with peppers and tomatoes in a flavorful summer salad.*

## INGREDIENTS

4 medium mackerel, about
8 ounces each, filleted
2 small red onions, cut into wedges
2 tablespoons chopped fresh
marjoram
4 tablespoons dry white wine
3 tablespoons olive oil
juice of 1 lime

FOR THE SALAD
1 red bell pepper
1 yellow bell pepper
1 small red onion
2 large plum tomatoes
1 tablespoon chopped fresh
marjoram
2 teaspoons balsamic vinegar
salt and freshly ground black
pepper

SERVES 4

**2** Mix together the marjoram, wine, oil and lime juice and spoon over the fish. Cover and chill in the refrigerator for at least 30 minutes, turning once.

**3** To make the salad, quarter and seed both peppers and halve the onion. Place the peppers and onion, skin side down, with the whole tomatoes on a hot grill and cook until the skins are blackened and charred.

**5** Chop the vegetables roughly and put them in a bowl. Stir in the marjoram and balsamic vinegar and season to taste. Toss thoroughly.

**6** Remove the kebabs from the refrigerator and cook on a hot grill for 10–12 minutes, turning occasionally and basting with the marinade. Serve with the pepper salad.

**1** Thread each mackerel fillet onto a skewer, with an onion wedge on each end. Arrange the skewers in a dish.

**4** Remove the vegetables from the grill and set aside until they are cool enough to handle. Use a sharp knife to peel off and discard the skins.

### Cook's Tip
Other oily fish can be used for this dish: try fillets or cubes of herring, rainbow trout or salmon, instead.

# VEGETARIAN
# &VEGETABLE
# DISHES

~

# VEGETABLE PARCELS WITH FLOWERY BUTTER

*Nasturtium leaves and flowers are edible and have a distinctive peppery flavor.*
*They make a pretty addition to a summer barbecue.*

## INGREDIENTS

*7 ounces baby carrots*
*9 ounces yellow pattypan squash*
*or summer squash*
*4 ounces baby corn*
*1 onion, thinly sliced*
*4 tablespoons butter, plus extra*
*for greasing*
*finely grated rind of ½ lemon*
*6 young nasturtium leaves*
*4–8 nasturtium flowers*
*salt and freshly ground*
*black pepper*

SERVES 4

**1** Trim the vegetables with a sharp knife, leaving them whole unless they are very large—if necessary, cut them into even-size pieces.

**2** Divide the vegetables among 4 double-thickness squares of buttered aluminum foil and season well.

**3** Mix the butter with the lemon rind in a small bowl. Roughly chop the nasturtium leaves and add them to the butter. Place a generous spoonful of the butter on each pile of vegetables in the squares of foil.

**4** Fold over the foil and seal the edges to make a neat parcel. Cook on a medium-hot grill for 30 minutes, until the vegetables are tender. Open the parcels and top each with one or two nasturtium flowers. Serve at once.

# SUMMER VEGETABLES WITH YOGURT PESTO

* * *

*Grilled vegetables make a meal on their own, or are delicious served as a
Mediterranean-style accompaniment to grilled meats and fish.*

### INGREDIENTS

2 small eggplants
2 large zucchini
1 red bell pepper
1 yellow bell pepper
1 fennel bulb
1 red onion
olive oil, for brushing
salt and freshly ground black
pepper

FOR THE YOGURT PESTO
⅔ cup strained plain yogurt
3 tablespoons pesto

SERVES 4

**2** Use a sharp kitchen knife to cut the zucchini in half lengthwise. Cut the peppers in half, removing the seeds but leaving the stalks in place.

**5** Arrange the vegetables on the hot grill, brush generously with olive oil and sprinkle with plenty of salt and freshly ground black pepper.

**1** Cut the eggplants into ½-inch slices. Sprinkle with salt and let drain for about 30 minutes. Rinse well in cold running water and pat dry.

**3** Slice the fennel bulb and the red onion into thick wedges, using a sharp kitchen knife.

**6** Cook the vegetables until golden brown and tender, turning occasionally. The eggplants and peppers will take 6–8 minutes to cook, the zucchini, onion and fennel 4–5 minutes. Serve the vegetables as soon as they are cooked, with the yogurt pesto.

**4** Stir the yogurt and pesto lightly together in a bowl, to make a marbled sauce. Spoon the yogurt pesto into a serving bowl and set aside.

### Cook's Tip
Baby vegetables make excellent candidates for grilling whole; look for baby eggplants and peppers, in particular. There's no need to salt the eggplants if they're small.

# GRILLED GOAT CHEESE PIZZA

• • •

*Pizzas cooked on the grill have a beautifully crisp and golden crust. The combination of goat cheese and red onion in this recipe makes for a flavorful main course dish.*

**2** Brush the dough round with olive oil and place, oiled side down, on a medium grill. Cook for 6–8 minutes, until firm and golden underneath. Brush the uncooked side with olive oil and turn the pizza over.

**3** Mix together the tomato sauce and pesto and quickly spread over the cooked side of the pizza, to within about ½ inch of the edge. Arrange the onion, tomatoes and cheese on top and sprinkle with salt and pepper.

### INGREDIENTS
*5-ounce package pizza-dough mix*
*olive oil, for brushing*
*⅔ cup tomato sauce*
*2 tablespoons tomato pesto*
*1 small red onion, thinly sliced*
*8 cherry tomatoes, halved*
*4 ounces firm goat cheese, thinly sliced*
*handful shredded fresh basil leaves*
*salt and freshly ground black pepper*

SERVES 4

**1** Make up the pizza dough according to the directions on the package. Roll out the dough on a lightly floured surface to a round about 10 inches in diameter.

**4** Cook the pizza for 10 minutes more, until golden brown and crisp. Sprinkle with fresh basil and serve.

# SWEET AND SOUR VEGETABLES WITH PANEER

° . °

*The Indian cheese used in this recipe, called paneer, can be bought at Asian stores, or you can use tofu in its place. Paneer has a good firm texture and cooks very well on the grill.*

## INGREDIENTS

1 green and 1 yellow bell pepper,
cut into squares
8 cherry, or 4 medium, tomatoes
8 cauliflower florets
8 fresh or canned pineapple chunks
8 cubes paneer

FOR THE SEASONED OIL
1 tablespoon soybean oil
2 tablespoons lemon juice
1 teaspoon salt
1 teaspoon freshly ground black
pepper
1 tablespoon honey
2 tablespoons chili sauce

SERVES 4

**1** Thread the prepared vegetables, pineapple and paneer cubes onto 4 skewers, alternating the ingredients.

**2** Mix together all the ingredients for the seasoned oil. If the mixture seems a little too thick, add 1 tablespoon water. Brush the vegetables with the seasoned oil.

**3** Cook on a hot grill or under the broiler for 10 minutes, turning the skewers often and basting with the seasoned oil. Sprinkle with pepper and serve on a bed of plain boiled rice.

# VEGETABLE KEBABS WITH PEPPERCORN SAUCE

• • •

*Vegetables invariably taste good when cooked on the grill. You can include other vegetables in these kebabs, depending on what is available at the time.*

### INGREDIENTS

· 24 mushrooms
16 cherry tomatoes
16 large fresh basil leaves
2 zucchini, cut into 16 thick slices
16 large fresh mint leaves
1 large red bell pepper, cut into
16 squares

TO BASTE
8 tablespoons (1 stick) melted
butter
1 garlic clove, crushed
1 tablespoon crushed green
peppercorns
salt

FOR THE GREEN PEPPERCORN SAUCE
4 tablespoons butter
3 tablespoons brandy
1 cup heavy cream
1 teaspoon crushed green
peppercorns

SERVES 4

**1** Thread the vegetables and herbs onto 8 bamboo skewers that have been soaked in water to prevent them from burning: Place the fresh basil leaves next to the tomatoes, and wrap the mint leaves around the zucchini slices.

**2** Mix the basting ingredients in a bowl and baste the kebabs thoroughly. Cook the skewers on a medium-hot grill, turning and basting regularly, until the vegetables are just cooked—this should take 5–7 minutes.

**3** Heat the butter for the green peppercorn sauce in a frying pan, then add the brandy and light it. When the flames have died down, stir in the cream and the peppercorns. Cook for 2 minutes, stirring constantly. Serve the sauce with the grilled kebabs.

# BAKED STUFFED ZUCCHINI

*The tangy goat cheese stuffing contrasts well with the very delicate flavor of the zucchini in this recipe. Wrap the zucchini in aluminum foil and bake them in the embers of the fire.*

**2** Insert pieces of goat cheese into the slits. Add a little chopped mint and sprinkle with the oil and black pepper.

**3** Wrap each zucchini in foil, place in the embers of the fire and bake for about 25 minutes, until tender.

### INGREDIENTS

*8 small zucchini, about*
*1 pound total weight*
*1 tablespoon olive oil, plus*
*extra for brushing*
*3–4 ounces goat cheese,*
*cut into thin strips*
*a few sprigs of fresh mint,*
*finely chopped, plus extra*
*to garnish*
*freshly ground black pepper*

SERVES 4

**1** Cut 8 pieces of aluminum foil large enough to encase each zucchini and lightly brush with olive oil. Trim the zucchini and cut a thin slit along the length of each.

#### Cook's Tip

While almost any cheese can be used in this recipe, mild cheeses, such as Cheddar or mozzarella, will best allow the flavor of the zucchini to be appreciated.

# STUFFED PARSLEYED ONIONS

*These stuffed onions are a popular vegetarian dish served with fresh crusty bread and a crisp salad. They also make a very good accompaniment to meat dishes.*

### INGREDIENTS

*4 large onions*
*4 tablespoons cooked rice*
*4 teaspoons finely chopped fresh parsley, plus extra to garnish*
*4 tablespoons finely grated sharp Cheddar cheese*
*2 tablespoons olive oil*
*1 tablespoon white wine*
*salt and freshly ground black pepper*

SERVES 4

**1** Cut a slice from the top of each onion and scoop out the center, leaving a fairly thick shell. Combine all the remaining ingredients in a large bowl and stir to mix, moistening with enough white wine to bind the ingredients together well.

**2** Use a spoon to fill the onions, then wrap each one in a piece of oiled aluminum foil. Bake in the embers of the fire for 30–40 minutes, until tender, turning the parcels often so they cook evenly. Serve the onions garnished with chopped fresh parsley.

# CORN ON THE COB IN A GARLIC BUTTER CRUST

*Whether you are catering for vegetarians or serving this with meat dishes, it will disappear in a flash. The charred garlic butter crust adds a new dimension to the corn.*

### INGREDIENTS

6 ears of fresh corn
½ pound (2 sticks) butter
2 tablespoons olive oil
2 garlic cloves, crushed
1 cup whole-wheat bread crumbs
1 tablespoon chopped fresh
parsley
salt and freshly ground black
pepper

SERVES 6

**1** Pull off the husks and silks and cook the corn in a large saucepan of boiling salted water until tender. Drain and set aside to cool.

**2** Melt the butter in a saucepan, add the olive oil, crushed garlic, salt and freshly ground black pepper, and stir to blend. Pour the mixture into a shallow dish. In another shallow dish blend the bread crumbs and chopped fresh parsley. Roll the corn in the melted butter mixture and then in the bread crumbs until they are well coated.

**3** Cook the corn on a hot grill for about 10 minutes, turning frequently, until the bread crumbs are golden brown.

# GRILLED EGGPLANT PARCELS

*These little bundles of tomatoes, mozzarella cheese and basil, wrapped in slices of eggplant, taste delicious cooked on the grill.*

### INGREDIENTS
2 large, long eggplants
8 ounces mozzarella cheese
2 plum tomatoes
16 large fresh basil leaves
2 tablespoons olive oil
salt and freshly ground black pepper

FOR THE DRESSING
4 tablespoons olive oil
1 teaspoon balsamic vinegar
1 tablespoon sun-dried tomato paste
1 tablespoon lemon juice

FOR THE GARNISH
2 tablespoons toasted pine nuts
torn fresh basil leaves

SERVES 4

**3** Cut the mozzarella cheese into 8 slices. Cut each tomato into 8 slices, not counting the first and last slices. Take 2 eggplant slices and arrange in a cross. Place a slice of tomato in the center, season, then add a basil leaf, followed by a slice of mozzarella, another basil leaf, another slice of tomato and more seasoning.

**4** Fold the ends of the eggplant slices around the filling to make a neat parcel. Repeat with the rest of the assembled ingredients to make 8 parcels. Chill the parcels in the refrigerator for about 20 minutes.

**5** To make the tomato dressing, whisk together the olive oil, vinegar, sun-dried tomato paste and lemon juice. Season to taste with plenty of salt and freshly ground black pepper.

**6** Brush the parcels with olive oil and cook on a hot grill for about 10 minutes, turning once, until golden. Serve hot, with the dressing, sprinkled with pine nuts and basil.

**1** Remove the stalks from the eggplants and cut them lengthwise into thin slices using a mandoline or long-bladed knife—aim to get 16 slices total, each about ¼ inch thick, not counting the first and last slices.

**2** Bring a large saucepan of salted water to the boil and cook the eggplant slices for about 2 minutes, until just softened. Drain the slices, then pat them dry on paper towels.

# POTATO WEDGES WITH GARLIC AND ROSEMARY

*Toss the potato wedges in fragrant, garlicky olive oil with chopped fresh rosemary,
before grilling them over the coals.*

### INGREDIENTS

*1½ pounds medium potatoes*
*1 tablespoon olive oil*
*2 garlic cloves, thinly sliced*
*4 tablespoons chopped fresh
rosemary*
*salt and freshly ground black
pepper*

SERVES 4

**1** Cut each potato into 4 wedges and parboil in boiling salted water for 5 minutes. Drain well.

**2** Toss the potatoes in the olive oil with the garlic, rosemary and black pepper. Arrange on a grill rack.

**3** Cook the potatoes on a hot grill for about 15 minutes, turning occasionally, until crisp and golden brown.

# POTATO SKEWERS WITH MUSTARD DIP

*Potatoes cooked on the grill have a good flavor and crisp skin.
These skewers are served with a thick, garlic-rich dip.*

## INGREDIENTS

*2¼ pounds small new potatoes
7 ounces shallots, halved
2 tablespoons olive oil
1 tablespoon sea salt*

FOR THE MUSTARD DIP
*4 garlic cloves, crushed
2 egg yolks
2 tablespoons lemon juice
1¼ cups extra virgin olive oil
2 teaspoons whole-grain mustard
salt and freshly ground black
pepper*

SERVES 4

**1** To make the mustard dip, place the garlic, egg yolks and lemon juice in a blender or food processor and process for a few seconds, until smooth.

**2** With the motor running, add the oil until the mixture forms a thick cream. Add the mustard and season.

**3** Parboil the potatoes in salted boiling water for about 5 minutes. Drain well and then thread them onto metal skewers with the shallots.

**4** Brush with olive oil and sprinkle with sea salt. Cook for 10–12 minutes over a hot grill, turning often, until tender. Serve with the mustard dip.

# DESSERTS

~

# SPICED PEAR AND BLUEBERRY PARCELS
. . .

*This fruity combination makes a delicious dessert for a hot summer evening.*
*You could substitute other berries for the blueberries if you prefer.*

### INGREDIENTS

4 firm, ripe pears
2 tablespoons lemon juice
1 tablespoon melted butter
1¼ cups blueberries
4 tablespoons light brown sugar
freshly ground black pepper

SERVES 4

**3** Cut 4 squares of double-thickness aluminum foil, large enough to wrap the pears, and brush them with melted butter. Place two pear halves on each, cut sides up. Gather the foil up around them, to hold them level.

**4** Mix the blueberries and sugar together and spoon them over the pears. Sprinkle with black pepper. Seal the edges of the foil over the pears and cook on a fairly hot grill for about 20–25 minutes.

**1** Peel the pears thinly. Cut them in half lengthwise. Scoop out the core from each half, using a teaspoon and a sharp kitchen knife.

**2** Brush the pears with lemon juice, to prevent them from discoloring.

### Cook's Tip

To assemble in advance, line with a layer of waxed paper, as the acid in the lemon juice may react with the foil and taint the flavor.

# GRILLED APPLES ON CINNAMON TOASTS

° ° °

*This simple, scrumptious dessert is best made with an enriched bread such as brioche,
but any light, sweet bread will do.*

### INGREDIENTS

*4 sweet dessert apples
juice of ½ lemon
4 individual brioches or muffins
4 tablespoons melted butter
2 tablespoons raw sugar
1 teaspoon ground cinnamon
whipped cream or strained plain
yogurt, to serve*

SERVES 4

**2** Cut the brioches or muffins into thick slices. Brush the slices with melted butter on both sides.

**4** Place the apple and brioche slices on a medium-hot grill and cook them for 3–4 minutes, turning once, until they are beginning to turn golden brown. Do not allow to burn.

**1** Core the apples and use a sharp knife to cut them into 3 or 4 thick slices. Sprinkle the apple slices with lemon juice and set them aside.

**3** Mix together the sugar and ground cinnamon in a small bowl to make the cinnamon sugar. Set aside.

**5** Sprinkle half the cinnamon sugar over the apple slices and brioche toasts and grill for another minute, until the sugar is sizzling and the toasts are a rich golden brown.

**6** To serve, arrange the apple slices over the toasts and sprinkle them with the remaining cinnamon sugar. Serve hot, with whipped cream or yogurt, if desired.

# PINEAPPLE WEDGES WITH RUM BUTTER GLAZE

° ° °

*Fresh pineapple is even more full of flavor when grilled, and this spiced rum glaze
makes it into a very special dessert.*

### INGREDIENTS

1 medium pineapple
2 tablespoons dark brown sugar
1 teaspoon ground ginger
4 tablespoons melted butter
2 tablespoons dark rum

SERVES 4

**3** Soak 4 bamboo skewers in water for 15 minutes to prevent them from scorching on the grill. Push a skewer through each wedge, into the stalk, to hold the chunks in place.

**4** Mix together the sugar, ginger, butter and rum and brush over the pineapple. Cook the wedges on the grill for 4 minutes; pour the remaining glaze over the top and serve.

**1** With a large, sharp knife, cut the pineapple lengthwise into 4 wedges. Cut out and discard the central core.

**2** Cut between the flesh and skin, to release the skin, but leave the flesh in place. Slice the flesh across and lengthwise to make thick chunks.

### Cook's Tip

For an easier version, simply remove the skin and then cut the whole pineapple into thick slices and cook as directed.

# NECTARINES WITH MARZIPAN AND MASCARPONE

○ ○ ○

*A luscious dessert that no one can resist—dieters may prefer to use low-fat cream cheese or
plain yogurt instead of mascarpone.*

### INGREDIENTS

4 firm, ripe nectarines or peaches
3 ounces marzipan
5 tablespoons mascarpone cheese
3 macaroons, crushed

SERVES 4

**1** Cut the nectarines or peaches in
half and remove the pits.

**2** Divide the marzipan into 8 pieces,
roll into balls, using your fingers, and
press one piece of marzipan into the pit
cavity of each nectarine half.

### Cook's Tip

Either nectarines or peaches can be
used for this recipe. If the pit does
not pull out easily when you halve
the fruit, use a small, sharp knife to
cut around it.

**3** Spoon the mascarpone cheese
on top of the fruit halves. Sprinkle
the crushed macaroons over
the mascarpone.

**4** Place the fruit halves on a hot grill
for 3–5 minutes, until they are hot and
the mascarpone starts to melt. Serve
immediately.

# ORANGES IN MAPLE AND COINTREAU SYRUP

∘ ∘ ∘

*This is one of the most delicious ways to eat an orange, and a luxurious way to round off a barbecue. For a children's or alcohol-free version, omit the liqueur.*

### INGREDIENTS

4 teaspoons butter, plus extra,
melted, for brushing
4 medium oranges
2 tablespoons maple syrup
2 tablespoons Cointreau or Grand
Marnier liqueur
crème fraîche or fromage frais,
to serve

SERVES 4

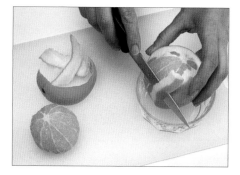

**2** Remove some shreds of orange rind, to decorate. Blanch these, dry them and set them aside. Peel the oranges, removing all the white pith and catching the juice in a bowl.

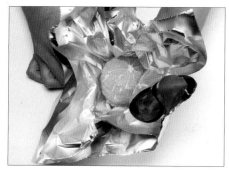

**4** Tuck the foil up securely around the oranges so that they keep their shape, leaving the foil open at the top.

**1** Cut 4 double-thickness squares of aluminum foil, large enough to wrap each of the oranges. Brush the center of each square of foil with plenty of melted butter.

**3** Slice the oranges crosswise into thick slices. Reassemble them and place each orange on a square of baking foil.

**5** Mix together the reserved orange juice, maple syrup and liqueur and spoon the mixture over the oranges.

**6** Add a pat of butter to each parcel and close the foil at the top to seal in the juices. Place the parcels on a hot grill for 10–12 minutes, until hot. Serve with crème fraîche or fromage frais, topped with the reserved shreds of orange rind.

# INDEX

. . .